DEDICATION

This book "My Friend, The Moon", Is a Hodge podge of the last several years. Hoping it leaves you with happy feelings, as you lead your everyday lives.

This will be my 11th book of mostly original, non-published writings since I started in 2006.

My thanks always to Judy "J" Elder, my editor and board to bounce ideas off of.

My profound Thanks to my mentor and friend, follow wordsmith Doug Hodges For your continued advice and support

My thanks to my publisher Cyberwit.net. The last sixteen years they have made it easy.

I want to thank my family - my wife and friend Kathy Newell, and parents John Everett and Dorothy Irene Newell.

I want to thank all my friends and co-workers who I have known through the years. You have lived in and between all the pages of my writings.

It is always my hope that I have left a measure of who I am and have been as a man and person in my writings. My intent is to allow future generations to know me somewhat, if they would want to.

I have re-invented myself many times now, in a lifespan of 68 years. I imagine I will keep doing that till the end! I'm still 18 at heart! Lastly, I need to give thanks to these most important people, who by their lives keep me living mine.

I love you Corey Everett Newell, Alissa Angeline (Newell) Staats

Nakoa Christopher Staats, Saige Corey Newell, Shawnee Angeline Staats, Ella Lynn Newell.

Thank You all from the bottom of my heart!

Thanks also to my son-in-law Rodney Staats, and my daughter in-law Jamie Newell

Anyway, Thanks to you all.

I remain,

The Big D

D Everett Newell

Bygd1@aol.com

Podcast Poet D Everett Newell

Contents

2nd Chances 9
1913 10
A First Poem 11
A Lone Sentinel 12
A Purity in Winter 13
A Question to God 14
A Question 15
A Tough Mantle 16
Alzheimer's 17
Anchor 19
Anger 20
Betcha Do 21
Bingo McGee 22
Bonfire 23
Bowels 25
Bracelet 26
Bucket List 27
Cake 28
CB Radio 29
Coal Mine 30
Cocoon 31
Colors 33
Copse of Trees 34
Covid-19 35
Culp's Hill 36
Cynical 37
Electro Glide 2021 39
Elvis the King is Gone 40
Embarrassing, Yeah, You Bet! 41

Fall is Upon Us	42
Family	43
Farm Living, or An Ode to Bigfoot	45
Feelings	46
Fog	47
Friend for Life?	48
Frustrated I Am	49
Going For a Walk	51
Grow	52
Hate	53
Hold Your Head High	54
How did you Know	55
How Do We Cope	56
Illness	57
I'm Empty	58
Impatient Man	60
Leader	61
Life	62
Lighthouses	64
Mailman Cometh	65
Mine to Keep	66
Mother's Day	67
My Deck of Cards	68
My Friend the Moon	69
My Lucky Sherm	70
New England	72
Nighttime Terrors	74
Out of My Depth	76
Poet's Horror	77
Saturday Morning	78
Seven Pillars	79
Skeletons	80
Soldiers of The Civil War	81

Solemn Promises 82
Soup 83
Sports Hurts 84
Sudden Loss 85
Sun 86
That's a Frustration 87
The Flood, At the Dobbins House 88
The Grim Reaper Covid 90
The Tough Mantel Of Life 91
This Mixed Jungle 92
This Problem 93
To Snack or Not 95
To 96
Travel Log 2021 97
Traveling Man 98
Trees, Now Gone 99
Trick or Treater 100
Type This 101
Vestibule 102
Wallet or A Murse 103
What a Mouth on Her 104
When Dear Friend's Disappears 105
Whimsy 106
Who is Albert Woolson, PT 2 107
Wondering Mind 109
Would Not 110
Yellow Balloon 111
Yonder 112
Slugger 114

2nd Chances

Do you remember
When we made mistakes
It was not a death knell
How many of us are perfect
Who does not have skeletons
In their closet

I remember a country
That believed in 2nd chances
A land where a misspoken word
Or a deed was forgiven
Where we could continue to live
A place you could reinvent

Why is it now, all we want
Is to destroy people, their legacies
A prevalent cancel culture
I would love to see a reboot
A coming together, united in forgiveness
Who is willing to take the first step

When I lay me down to sleep
Tossing and turning looking to dream
But I can't, but I want to
I am filled with hope
The day will come once again
Our lives can include 2nd chances

D Everett Newell 2/11/2021

1913

Chamberlaine sat upon a jaded rock
Memories rushed back
To this now old man
He winced as he adjusted his body
Wound still aggravated from the Great War
A war of rebellion
One started to down slavery
To free fellow men from their oppression
The years had flown by
So much so it was hard to fathom
His life was filled with achievement
On this day, sitting there
Sitting in those woods
His eyes filled with tears
He wiped hem with a sleeve
Hoping no one would notice
They, he, had lost so much
Brothers in arms had died
So many now a whisper in his mind
He could still see the men fall
As each new grey wave hit them
But they held, they held the left flank
They had done it, the day was won
Knowing this would probably be
His last visit to this now sacred spot
Bowing his head down in prayer
Lifting his aged body up
Saying one last good-bye

D Everett Newell 2/26/2021

A First Poem

Ok I am writing again
Not knowing where It,
will end
But the beginning is fun
When the piece is done,
I will hit send
Here I am, hitting the keyboard
Stroke after stroke
Trying to find a cadence
So, my readers are not bored
The smallest of ideas
Seeping from my soul
Sometimes flowing slowly
Others, A torrential rain
Poetry comes in waves
Crashing unto, then from my brain
Some while gazing out a window
Others at night in my dreams
A commonality they share
And a coming they must
A personal conduit
From somewhere,
Their identity unknown
For all of you to read
And for me to continually bleed

D Everett Newell   11/10/2019

A Lone Sentinel

I hear a pitter patter
Sitting at my perch
Looking out a window
The rain falls slowly
Deliberately, soaking all in its wake
No birds or animals in site
People staying with safe spaces
Trees, bushes, grass soaking it up
One of those moments life stands still
Like waiting for a next breath
Anticipating the coming charge
Yet all on pause, the rain drops
Getting a bit disillusioned
Maybe a tad depressed
Riveted, I look for something
Anything to break this conundrum
Then I see it, I breath deep
A single, large, beautiful
Pink Hibiscus opened up
Drinking a drink of moisture
Quenching a thirst thereby
Lifting up all within sight
Thanks, to a Lone Sentinel

D Everett Newell 9/22/2021

A Purity in Winter

The cold wind takes our breath away
Frigid is in our souls and the air
Walking brings a distinct cracking
Hard to get moving, my cement bones
Do not work, and I slip and slide
Yet I move on, longing for the sun
Four seasons are always a human test
We get to pass, four times a year
Now looking around, there are no
Green grasses, red yellow flowers
Life of the summer gone, our yard barren
There is a renewal of survival
Birds gather near our feeders
Squirrels underneath catching their spillage
Deer track deep abound in the snow
Our world is frozen, not dead
I see the beauty, a purity in winter

D Everett Newell 2/12/2021

A Question to God

Why does human hair
Grow ten times faster
In every direction
In my ears, nose,
Even on my back
Yet not a blade nor thread
Upon my very bald, and shiny dome
A place I'd really like it
Would that be too much to ask
Too much of an effort
Come on, really,
Please explain to me,
The justice of it all
Go on,
 Just one simple reason
Seems it would be easy
For your omnipotent presence
To one who created all
A very simple task, really
To put hair on our heads
Bare on all other places
Can I get an "Amen"?

D Everett Newell 9/21/2021

A Question

I used to ask
One burning question
Will you be with me
In the end
I now know
That is a wrong question
Hypocritical of me
To think in that way
A more important realization
Will you
Be with me, while I live
Slaying life's problems
Systematically every day
Beside me,
Rather this then the alternative
Plastically celebrating me
Once I am gone
Don't appear after my last breath
Exclaiming to all,
What a great person I was
So, I now ask
A better question
Will you be with me
While I live?

D Everett Newell 11/11/2019

A Tough Mantle

When you get a call for help
From someone you deeply care about
But your choices are limited
In any meaningful way
What can you do
When you can't find a substantive answer
Hearing the pain in others voices
Wears upon your heart, troubling the soul
Trying everything from humor to tears
Hoping somehow to break thru
A formidable wall
All understanding disappearing at each hello
A person disappearing every hour of every day
Shared memories now one sided and obsolete
Praying for answer, knowing there are none
Can only stand by, watch this play out
Yet you keep on thru the anger and confusion
Trying to connect again and again and again
People matter, they're worth struggling for,
And completely giving them the compassion
They thru a long well lived life have earned
This is the tough mantle of life!

D Everett Newell 4/24/2021

Alzheimer's

I hate you
I hate what you do to people
You take away everything
Because of you

They forget what they want to say
They forget where they are at
They forget who we are
They lose all everyday functionality

Can't cook
Can't Eat
Can't drink
Can't take medicines

I hate you
I hate what you do to people
You rob everything
Because of you

They are robbed of their identity
They are robbed of their self-worth
They are robbed of their memories
They are robbed of rightful emotions
They are plainly robbed of a life

Can't cook
Can't Eat

Can't drink
Can't take medicines

Alzheimer's
I hate you
I hate what you do to people
You take away everything

D Everett Newell 11/11/2019

Saige Corey Newell

Anchor

You are there
For me always
Steadfast
In support
A weight in that flood
Keeping me
From drifting away

Support
A Ying to my Yang
Loved needed cherished
Filling my heart
A soulmate
Trusted friend
I so want
To be the same for you

I am always there
Always thinking
Trying to support
Amid bad decisions
A weight
In that flood
Hopefully not
Dragging you down to drown

Always an anchor
Both good
And the bad

D Everett Newell 9/17/2021

Anger

Seething it forms
Seething it builds
Seething it hurts
Seething it explodes

Anger needs controlled
Needs channeled, needs understood

Seething it feeds
Seething it controls
Seething it pushes
Seething it grabs

Anger unchecked controls
Unchanneled energy, no understanding

Calming averts crises
Calming makes humanity
Calming makes sense
Calming anger necessary

Simply no good, for anything
      Anger stands alone!
      Hurts us all
      Anger!

D Everett Newell 9/16/2021

Betcha Do

Do you like competition
Do you like money
I have a proposition for you
Baseball, football, basketball
Any kind of ball
It's called taking a chance
You plop down your dollars
Or cents if you have any sense
Grabbing the right odds
Multiply your grass stakes
There are the losses
Oh yeah, many losses
But the pie in the sky
Begs you, cajoles you on
Lotteries of all kinds
Twenty-four seven, all hours
Onward you trek to that elusive goal
The Big One, The Life Changing One
A ghost of a chance
I'll keep taking my turns
Do you want to join me?
I Betcha Do!

D Everett Newell 2/20/2021

Bingo McGee

Let me start
By telling you a short story
He was by all accounts
A very strange man
The one and only
Bingo McGee
Being a Modern-day hero
He loved to fly
Being an extraordinary guy
Over tall hills,
And low hanging clouds
Higher that anything else can
A rocking roller-coaster
Against deep blue skies
His billowing smoke
A whiter than white trail
Let me start
By telling you a short story
He was by all accounts
A very strange man
This living legend, Bingo McGee
Always the hero,
I mean he could be nothing less
Even in the worst of days
He surely passed the test
Not fitting any latter day normal
A failure some would say
Yet a legend to many
To know him was to love him
A living doll

D Everett Newell 11/12/2019

Bonfire

We stacked the dry wood
Just as
The sun set
Stars were beginning
To show themselves
Moon starting
Its silver illuminance
One single match
Put against the kindling
Fire is funny
It takes a bit
Then slowly
It takes hold progressing
It's now an unstoppable
Unmovable force
In our fire pit
It's a captured animal
Moving back and forth
Licking its lips
We can visually
See its power
Warmth starts to envelope us
And the smoke
Wafts upward
Now it's flickering
Orange, yellow, blue
So destructive
But in its present form
It soothes us

Relaxes us
We're lucky
To be here
In the moment
Time sitting
Dreaming
Near a bonfire

D Everett Newell 10/2/2021

Gettysburg, PA

Bowels

Down in the bowels
Hard helmet and filtered light
Spent many long and cold bakelite nights
Down in the bowels
Cart after cart I put away
Should have looked like Popeye
Homesick, 12 hours alone
Plays with your mind
Joints creak now and ache
Years of heavy lifting, but wait
I got out of those bowels
Left the bats and hard floor
Write about them now, remember
Forever more
Down in the bowels
Hard helmet and filtered light
Spent many long and cold nights

D Everett Newell 9/23/2021

Bracelet

Sitting in the home alone
A bleak day, one of many
In a year of darkness
Of isolation and loneliness
Staring off into her dreams
A man tapped on her shoulder
Holding bouquets of flowers
A wrist corsage around a shiny silver bracelet
She smiled and eyes lit up
For the first time
In a very long time
A tear, confused look
Questioning, why me, why now?
Said to her, because it was time
Loving that bracelet
Led her thru that long period
One that killed many
We her family, cried
Hearing the excitement in Mom's voice
Making us, her family, feel good
Knowing for that moment
She was not alone
Wearing that beautiful bracelet

D Everett Newell 4/4/2021

Bucket List

I have had mine
Do you have a wish list of life targets?
Yeah I've had many
Well maybe one list that ebbs and flows
Multitudes of ads and subtractions
I got, the hunting, fishing,
The driving, motorcycle, licenses
A gun permit, bought several homes,
Been to tons of great music concerts.
Had girlfriends, married twice, have two great kids,
Four wonderful grandkids!
Visited places I never thought I'd see
Worked 40-plus years, retired on my own terms
Too many friends to count
So what's left on my list?
The more whimsical wants
Got to get to Woodstock, Bethel, and Saugerties NY
Have to see the Big Pink
Got to get to Point Pleasant, West Virginia,
To the Mothman Festival
Things that can be crossed off,
 My expanding bucket list

D Everett Newell 5/18/2021

Cake

Desert? Yes, No, Oh Yeah Man!
Some like it chocolate
Some vanilla
Icings can be many colors
So many flavors
They can look like a picture
Designed to resemble
Your favorite pet or person
If you like to bake
The world is your pallet
Both taste and imagination
Helping us celebrate
All kinds of occasions
Or just because of a sweet tooth
Nothing like this building
Of sugar, eggs and flours
Also combined with ice cream
Provides a unique culinary treat
So much to be desired
In something so simple to make
This was written to show
Honor to a delicious cake

D Everett Newell 2/25/2021

CB Radio

Back in the day, moons ago
We drove around in our cars
Hours upon hours just talking away
In this foreign tongue of the CB radio
Citizen Band the Government called it
It was us alone under the moonlit skies
Oh and the hundreds of people
Who were on the airwaves any given night
So much money spent on putting gas in the tanks
Calling out, "breaker, breaker", "hey good buddy"
"You got your ears on?" and then,
 Waiting for a static answer
Then hearing, "You got him, over"
So many handle names, as we went on
 We lost our government license code names
Soba Boy, Deputy Dog, became our aliases.
Spending so much time with the likes of
Red Beard, Medina Dreamer and Knowlsville Gopher!
It really was a simpler time but owned its own magic
I miss those days, I miss my friends who
Made up this mystical CB world, so for now
"This is Mr. Confusion, I'm signing off,
One last time!"

D Everett Newell 2/25/2021

Coal Mine

Somewhere in the hills of PA
During the early turn of the 20th Century
A young man, a boy really
Suddenly is thrust into manhood
With his family's world
Squarely upon his shoulders
He dons a lighted hardhat
Grabs his pick and shovel
Walks down that long dark rock tunnel
He is twelve, his father had just died
A mine cave-in took him
Leaving this family destitute
Now he realizes it's up to him
He is the oldest, no choices left
Almost everything he earns
In that dirty, dusty work
Is owed to the company store
Which is owned by the mine
The same that took his Dad
Now owns him and his family
This is not fiction, this is his story
The story of Adam Carr
I know this, he was my Granddad
And his times were defined
By the coal mines of PA

D Everett Newell 9/22/2021

Cocoon

Where did she go
One minute running around playing
Coming thru my front door
With a Hi Papa,
What are there for snacks
Forever my Batman
Suddenly,
My adorable little girl
Erupted from her shell
Emerging as this beautiful young lady
Seeing the excitement in her voice
On being asked to the prom
My heart burst with pride
Tears welled up in my eye's.
Knowing the transition to adult
Being well underway
Her prom dress is stunning.
She demands it be that way
This girl glows, with a certain radiance
Not to be denied,
In a year that much was
This class of 2021 has missed a lot
Covid had robbed them,
Yet they are resilient and steadfast
Ready to greet the world,
As they march on
Can't speak for them all
But this girl, will be fine
She can't help herself,

A bright light in our world
Graduation lays now at her door
And the last vestiges of childhood
Disappearing as final maturing occurs
As painful as it is to me
I have to share my secret now
As this wonderful person
Emerges from her cocoon

D Everett Newell 5/2/2021

Gettysburg, PA

Colors

As I sit here, upon my perch
Viewing a breathtaking palette of hues
Our world on full display
A smorgasbord of retinal delights
Wavy white puffy clouds
Slowly moving above
Swimming through a very blue pool
Of earth's nicest sky
Brown trees poking through a
Green pasture of lawns
As their branches once more
Come alive, erupting again
Man's trappings share nature's portrait
With his buildings, cars, toys of every shade
So mundane, yet filled with
Excitement of sunny everyday life
Glad I can experience
These magnificent colors

D Everett Newell 5/18/2021

Copse of Trees

15,000 arranged as if on parade
Marching toward a sure death
As men dropped from the various
Shot, shell, bullets raining on them
Men would jump in
Filling the wounded's places
Gaps in the dying lines
Non-wavering, on they went
Power in their might, toward
A singular spot, the target
In the union line
The smoky haze, enveloped all
Smells of Sulphur, of lead
Of death, permeated everything
Courage never seen before
Probably not again
A gray wave in unity
Moved toward that copse of trees
To their annihilating end

D Everett Newell 5/18/2021

Covid-19

You came in hot
Like a tidal wave
Or life altering tsunami
Changing everything in your wake
You essentially wiped out a full year
Taking everything in your path
Globally leaving nothing as it was
You wiped out schools
You wiped out concerts
You wiped out sports
You took lives away
You took families away
You took our promise away
Now as we vaccinate
All we have left is a hope
Memories of all we lost
Trying to once again move forward
Our economy damaged
Struggling now to regain
We will never forget you
Try as we might
Hoping to say finally
Good-Bye to Covid-19

D Everett Newell 2/19/2021

Culp's Hill

A sharp left turn
Brings us to the base
As the sun rises
Defining shapes through
The early morning fog
Shadows take on
Lives of their own
This is a mystic mound
A road from purgatory
Rebel and Yank took
To their final heaven
We wind upward
From the base
Curve after curve we rise
So quiet now, so horrific then
Limbs, splintered from shot
Ground heaved open upon shell
So peaceful now
A new dawn of Death, then
I can hear screams of pain
The Rebel Yell in charge
Furiously this battle ebbed
Blue, Gray, Gray, then Blue
Hand to hand they fought
Savages beating each other
To this world's last end
I now look, wonder
Thinking, amazing, as I once more
Climb this Culp's Hill

D Everett Newell 10/4/2021

Cynical

I used to be a dreamer
Always first to see
The silver lining
Usually the first
To give a second chance
Believing in my worst days
Tomorrow better
Even in the pouring rain
A rainbow will come
The sun will shine
After our greatest storms
Our tears will drip dry
Given some time
My aches will disappear
Tomorrow
I'll see everyone I've lost
In the future
Being a forever optimist
Is how I lived
This world I'm afraid
Has beaten me
I'm bruised
Have chinks in my armor
I'm bent
Not yet broken
I'm so very tired
I need a recharge
Help me
Please help me

Our world now so depressing
So much cold
Greed, selfishness
Lost in this quagmire
Of a "Me" world
Fighting to right
My own self-being
Averting emotional overloads
Tring my very best
To quit being cynical

D Everett Newell 9/28/2021

Shawnee Staats, Gettysburg, PA

Electro Glide 2021

Off the elevator they came
Elderly man with a cane
Then she appeared, a blur
Blazing by, what I assume
Was her partner, her attendee
In a short powered wheelchair
Bobbing in and out, swerving with power
Making a statement
A diminutive older woman
Sitting in the command chair
Wrapped up in the trappings of winter
Oxygen to her nose
Stocking cap from head to ears
Obviously a frail person
Well physically, her appearance
Showed spirit and independence
Managing to back into the waiting room
To a space unoccupied
Touching as her caregiver
Tenderly unwrapped her outer protection
As I looked, he took his hand
To hers, gently removing and straightening
And massaging her fingers free
From the wheelchair control pad
What a striking pair they made
Touching my heart
This lady friend on the
Electro Glide 2021

D Everett Newell 3/2/2021

Elvis the King is Gone

One day, a mid-August day
In my car I was riding
Of course my radio was full on
It was a typical summer day
Hot, hazy, humid, a sticky day
One hit after another
Played the rock station's loop
Then I heard, seems like this morning
"We now break into this programming"
This was, this is, always a sign
One of dread, weary expectation
"We have just learned", crackled on
"In Memphis, Elvis has died"
No last name, no need
Everyone on this planet
Knew of Elvis Presley, The King
He of the energized sexual movements
One of the most cultural icons
Of my life, of the 20th century
His interpretation of song
Showed with potency
A mix that influenced
Across all racial barriers
Elvis The King was gone!
The moment I heard of his death
I looked in the rearview mirror
Staring at me, my own curled lip

D Everett Newell 10/5/2021

Embarrassing, Yeah, You Bet!

Let me ask, have you that one moment
The one that got away
And the one you want back
I think we all have a least one
If being completely honest, many
Have you ever leaned on a locker
Changing clothes, how was I to know
It was not hooked to wall, which
Set off a cascading tsunami that toppled
Every locker in the room, lucky now one was killed
Have you ever gone to your first college class
And spoke to your female teacher,
As Miss Chesty, her name was Cheasty
Whoops I'd like that one back
Have you ever danced on a table
To the infamous song "Disco Duck"
Only to have table split in two
And subsequently asked to leave the establishment
Have you ever been led out
Of Goat Island in the Niagara Falls
Because you did not know Park closed at 11
I also saw a car wreck outside of a bar
In Batavia NY, but was a bit to inebriated to help
When Police questioned as a witness to it
Looking back now, I'm a bit mortified and I promise
These are only a few times I've done stupid things
Things that seemed to make sense at the time
Now, they are embarrassing yeah,, you bet!

D Everett Newell 4/26/2021

Fall is Upon Us

Leaves once again, turning colors
Soon dropping to the ground
Squirrels very excited, scamp around

Wind's back and gaining momentum
Each day brings more dark, less light
Fall is now in the air, a coolness abounds

Noticing people now bundled up
The days of T-shirts and shorts gone
We've turned that corner, where winter belongs

Clouds slowly change from puffy white
To light and dark grey
Trees almost barren again

To make matters worse
Our 24 hour clocks reset
Losing more of our active time

Lastly pumpkins, apples in abundance
Scary faces march through the night
Ghoulishly funny as winter nears

Seasons change, we adjust
Having no choice, we're along for the ride
Again, that time where fall is upon us

D Everett Newell 2/26/2021

Family

That building block
That binds us,
 Making us stronger
The cement of life
We laugh, play
We cry together
When all else fails
Family is, they will always be
A trusted fall back
Supporting me thru a divorce
Through two marriages
Through birth's
 As well as numerous Deaths
Because of them
I do proceed through life
My head always held high
Because of them,
 My self-worth is evident
They have nurtured and protected me
My confidence built
 Because of their support
Allowing me to be me
Through everyday trials and errors
Loving me always,
Even thru my many mistakes
Thus, allowing me to rebound
Each time, a bit healthier and wiser
Adding to personal assimilation and
Individual growth

Becoming the person, I am
With the guiding light
Of Family

D Everett Newell 11/13/2019

Gettysburg, PA

Farm Living, or An Ode to Bigfoot

I went out to Farmer Dell's
Only wanted to look into his well
Bending over, I heard such a scream
So much, old man Dell, stepped in his cream
The cat and dog's did scurry
My own legs tried making off in a hurry
Never did I expect, to see this sight
Bigfoot howling with all his might
His dark brown matted hair
Was awash with something there
Confused more then angry he looked around
Fear gripping me, still laughed at this clown
Life froze all things for the moment, nothing moved
Then looking around, I saw him dance his groove
I saw on that big block of a face a slight grin
Myself relaxing, walking slowing toward him
As quick as he appeared he was poof, gone
My ode to this experience now captured, and lives on

D Everett Newell 4/24/2021

Feelings

We all get them, Feelings
Sometimes things hurt or dismay
For that I've nothing to say

We all get them, Feelings
Frustrated, no explanation why
Tears well up, eyes redden, I cry

We all get them, Feelings
People ponder, I can't
Losing control, I vocally rant

We all get Feelings, we get hurt, angry, confused
We sometimes, without willingness
Give in to our Feelings!

We all get them, Honest we do
You can't ignore, Feelings

D Everett Newell 9/20/2021

Fog

Swallowing me up
Suffocating, it moves in
Taking away smell, sight, sound
This grey fog captures all
It's heavy, thick, omnipresent
My skin crawls with its dew
I walk faster, and then faster

Looking for a way out
Lights in the distance
Burn through its thickness, yet
All seems dead, muted, eerie
What hell have I entered?
Pulse picks up, heartbeat in my ears
I walk faster, then faster

I start to shake, tremble
Water cascading on my cheeks
Salt taste now lights upon my lips
As they begin to rapidly quiver
Now into a steady rhythmic run
Picking up speed, yet going nowhere

Pulse picks up to the drum of my heart
Suddenly I stop, no way out of this
Darkness closes in around me, no way out
Chest tightness as it envelops, heavy, nasty
My world gone, entering a new realm
Fear overcomes no way out of this
Encapsulating fog!

D Everett Newell 9/22/2021

Friend for Life?

When we make that moral contract
Integrity demands we honor it
The term friend,
That contract then is for life
Is it used meaningfully?
Or is it used possibly carelessly
Is there a way to judge this state?
A friend for life, Lets exam
Who gets to purview it?
At life's end
Who then is the judge?
Let the chips fall where they must
Consistency hopefully will dictate
Those who stood with us,
Or those that did not
If luck,
 Hopefully is on our side
We made good life decisions
On whom we surrounded
Ourselves with
Thru life's ups and downs
If we stood together thru
The trials and tribulations
Good and BAD,
That would prove to sit forever
On the mantel of friends for life

D Everett Newell 11/12/2019

Frustrated I Am

Frustrated, Yes I am
Division is everywhere
In today's world
Under every rock
Around every corner
Compassion, empathy
Are in short order

Why can't our populace
Be simpler and kinder
Why does every miscue
Get magnified a thousand times
I'm short on understanding
Common sense shattered
Into so many jagged shards
And forget street sense
Nobody tries to fit in
Instead, expecting a selfishness
A greed unlike ever before
It's a total 'Me' society
It's the only thing that matters
Solo we stand without reproach
Alone hands, yet handouts for everything
Screw thy neighbor
Grab what's yours

I just want to see, generosity
Once again, a Piece of Peace
Let's get back,

Maybe to the Prince of Peace
We all need to heed
We all need to start
Looking out for our brothers and sisters
We must become unified once more
Set societal common goals again

D Everett Newell 10/9/2021

Gettysburg, PA

Going For a Walk

Early morning, out my door
I step into a brisk
But sunny day, beauty bursts forth
Slowly to take in nature's wonder
I keep pace to my soul's drummer
As my shoes clod along the way
This is man's simple pleasure
Costs no money, needs no equipment
Just pick a direction
Letting your imagination run wild
Our world is mine to investigate
To be alone with my self
Chances to sort out thoughts
Or make plans, or just soak all in
Wondrous is this trek of the ordinary
I know these smells and noises
Yet still resplendent in the mundane
Opening to all its possibilities
Honest to a fault, I feel alive
Now something odd stirs me
As I open my eyes, still in bed
Jumping up, throwing on clothes
Thinking, I'm going for a walk

D Everett Newell 2/25/2021

Grow

Some days start out great
Others seem
Like you're walking in quicksand
Getting no traction
As hard as you might
Like a thousand broken mirrors
Jagged hours pass slowly
Try to get to bedtime
Hoping a reset can right
No choice but to deal
Dragging through, everyone has one
It's not personal
Still makes you blue
Respite will come, this test
Will be won, history shows us
With a life lived
We will conquer, continue
To grow!

D Everett Newell 5/19/2021

Hate

Seeing it on TV, Hate
Seeing it on social media, Hate
Hate funnels down
From the Presidency
Filtering downward through Congress
To our local municipalities, Hate
Hate funnels down
Our society no longer
Turns the other cheek, Hate
Parents have harder edges
Funneling to children, Hate
Hate, Hate, Hate
Say it one more time, Hate

Are you as sick of it as I am
Let's be kinder, gentler
More understanding
Realize all people of every race
All nationalities, are mostly decent
We all live in glass houses
Quit throwing stones
Please, Please Stop
    The Hate!

D Everett Newell 10/6/2021

Hold Your Head High

When you walk
    Hold Your Head High
When you talk
    Hold Your Head High
When you look
    Hold Your Head High
When you breathe
    Hold Your Head High

Have a stride strong
An appearance that stirs
Beam with confidence
Believe in who you are
Show what you'll become
Others will follow where you lead
Charisma covers scars of life

Hold Your Head High
Hold Your Head High

When you breathe
When you walk
When you look
When you talk
Hold Your Head High!

D Everett Newell   9/27/2021

How did you Know

Was it something I said?
Was it the way I looked?
Was it my face turning red?
How did you know

Why do I now feel guilty?
Why do you see inside me?
Why do I care so much, what you think?
How did you know

Who told you?
Who would betray me?
Who thought that about me?
How did you know

D Everett Newell 11/15/2019

How Do We Cope

Mother-Son flips to a
Daughter-Father relationship
Age, dementia, tipped the scale
A balancing act, neither of us
Prepared for, or are good at!
Patience is needed, yet
We both run on empty
Questions then answers
Then questioning of the answers
Round and round we go
Playing whack-a-mole
With a fading memory
A life lived becomes a puzzle
All the pieces remain
But forced together, in
Patterns that make no logical sense
We carry on, trying to communicate
But always a lingering, burning question of
How do we cope?

D Everett Newell 5/16/2021

Illness

When young, usually no thinking
No thinking of sickness or
Anything about pain or difficulty
Getting through each day
Of course there is a percentage
Always a percentage of young are sick
For the most part, it's an older person
Affliction, or afflictions
It's sick to feel sick
You know what I mean
Every day a chore to get through
Walking or wanting to get to sleep
And going to bed too tired to wake up
The hours between morning and nighttime
Filled with pain, coughing
Schedule of meds, foods, etc.
Sometimes you feel like eating
Other times you just do not
Hard to focus, to think
Praying for a good day or days
Tired of living like this
So tired, So tired, But carry on
I must carry on, as do you
Can't fall prey or give in to
Illness!

D Everett Newell 2/19/2021

I'm Empty

Very now and then, comes a day
Where we take inventory of ourselves
Staring into the mirror of oneself
Not always a great assessment or reflection
Today is one of those days,
Having done so, now I feel empty
No hope, well some, but no light
Certainly don't feel whole
Have you had those days
Where you are here,
 But also way over there
I hear, feel, but yet in a dream
Or is it a nightmare, can't be sure
My brain constantly
 Fighting my heart and soul
Wanted better, but to be honest
Better can't be defined
What the hell is this better
Surrounded by loving family and friends
Always feeling a piece missing
Not allowing a peace within
Can't buy happiness, I've tried
Can't eat your way to feeling great
God knows I have tried that as well
What is wrong with me
Somebody speak up, I need to find
Answers within myself, but can't
Really could use a clue
If you have an idea, would you

I decided to put down on paper
What I can't verbally articulate
My passion has gone, stone cold
As I read back to myself
Still nothing electric,
 Looks back at me
Always searching for astounding
 Nothing ever changes,
Settling for the mundane
Having to get a well needed charge
Yet I will keep at it, well
You know what, it's time,
My conduit battery has died
Nothing else left to give,
Done trying to continue on
I just can't, I'm empty

D Everett Newell 5/3/2021

Dedicated to all who feel isolated, not whole, remember your never alone! Ever!

Impatient Man

I'm just an impatient man
It's really who I am

I don't like lose ends
Mostly see in black and white trends

I like and trust what I can see
Void of this, then I'll leave it be

I like and trust what I can touch
Not doing so pisses me off and such

I'm no tomorrow man
Needing a straightforward plan

I'm just an impatient man
It's really who I am

D Everett Newell 9/17/2021

Leader

Our leaders anymore
Don't leave us secure
In any rationale
They do not represent
The best of us
Most are driven by
Power, greed, notoriety
They all live in glass houses
Afraid of which stones we shall throw
Instead, they work to divide us
In division, we don't notice
All of the stupidity in their rule
And it is a rule
We might as well adjust
To many new normals
Integrity is earned through
Consistency, which always remains
In that direct correlation
To a credibility of sorts
Today's leaders have none
They might as well be naked
Because the facade they project
Is worthless to the whole
Maybe the word leader
Being an oxymoron

D Everett Newell 3/4/2021

Life

We as a species, a human one
Desire to live, as long as possible
Granted, we remain relatively healthy
Relatively have a quality of life
At some point most of us know
When the end is near, not always
But we sort of make peace with death
Not necessarily giving up
Yet readying for an end!

They as a species, a canine one
Desire to live, as long as possible
They don't have a gauge to check health
Keeping on regardless of quality of life
Seemingly, they don't know
An end nears, life becomes more difficult
Never making peace of giving in
Or giving up the struggle to survive
Not realizing there's an end.

Seeing it in their faces
Seeing their daily struggles
Seeing no eyesight or hearing
Seeing difficulty in walking
Seeing difficulty in eating

We must make that decision
It Hurts! It Hurts!
Deciding to save them
By ending their life

D Everett Newell 3/15/2021

Classic Car, Western, NY

Lighthouses

Waves crash upon the stone
Your facing does get the surge
Water, sometimes ice, batters you
Yet you stand, once a beacon
To warn huge transport ships
Of inherent dangers close to land
Representing mostly a bygone era
We still honor your presence
Dotted all along the Great Lakes
You are historic markers
Of the Great Industrial Age
Guiding monstrous ships
Through dangerous waters to safety
Now your glory is captured
On film, digital, occasional postcard
Looking at all of them
I'm moved to catch that glimpse
Of the spiraled building
With the large rotating light
A guardian of yesteryear
So thankful for all of the lighthouses

D Everett Newell 3/13/2021

Mailman Cometh

I hear that motored noise
Emanating down our street
No mistaking that sound
It is our mail
Today's surprises on their way
Making the last beeline to box
Pickup and opening
What mysteries are bestowed today

I hear that motored noise
Emanating down our street
An experience six times weekly
Bills, payment, toys, and such
Surprises from friends, especially neat
Can't wait to open, anticipation building
Another clockwork like day
Thanks to this diligent worker

I'm so grateful
When the mailman cometh, then
The motored noise slowly
Becomes, smaller and smaller
The mailman goeth, away

D Everett Newell 10/5/2021

Mine to Keep

The bright sun gets to my eyes
I kick off the covers, ready to rise

Breakfast awaits, but before, a trek
Stretching my arms, legs, torso, and neck

First steps hurt, a bit of dismay
But never mind, on I go to start my day

I have a list today of accomplishments
Of course, unknown waters always sent

Onward I go, as fast as I might
The clock ticks on, my speed bites

Frustrated, the sun waves me a final "Adieu"
So another day passed, comes with drops of dew

Sitting in my oversized thinking chair
Twenty-four hours, most fast, it's a scare

Laying down now, my eyes close to sleep
Memories of past nightmares, dreams, mine to keep

D Everett Newell 9/22/2021

Mother's Day

Mothers are the nurturers
Mothers are family pillars
Mothers smile when they feel like crying
Mothers go without sleep
Mothers go without eating
Mothers just do what they need to

Mothers are the nurturers
Mothers are our family's glue
Mothers ignore when they are filled with pain
Mothers go without to clothe us
Mothers go without new things
Mothers just do what they need to

A bastion of protection
A fort to our fears
They teach us, humanize us
No one would exist without them
Let's always remember
Even when they can't
The love they've shown for all of us

Mothers are the nurturers
Mothers are family pillars
Mothers smile when they feel like crying
Mothers go without sleep
Mothers go without eating
Mothers just do what they need to

D Everett Newell 5/9/2020

My Deck of Cards

We all hold them
Most of us need them
Through life we win
With these best hands of life

King are the patriarch of family
Queens the supporting set, the matriarchs
Jokers being the siblings
Cousins, aunts, and uncles
Then the many number cards
Making up all other relatives and friends

We all hold them
Most of us need them
Through life we win
With these best hands of life

Being dealt with specific hands
As we proceed through time
We define what we hold
What we decide to throw away
Which new card drawn to our hand
Aces special, are rare unforgettable people

We all hold them
Most of us need them
Through life we win
When we make our best hands of life

D Everett Newell 10/6/2021

My Friend the Moon

My young friend always looked to the sky
Pointed is very small finger upward
Exclaiming to all, look up there
I see my friend the moon
He would laugh a very cute giggle
As he was all cute at this age
In his best little kid voice
Smiling radiantly from one ear to the other
This memory constantly reminds me
Of another time, one more simple
Where happiness, was to simply look skyward
Seeing the twinkling of stars
Our fully lit Moon
And feeling alive, watching my Grandson
His awe for what we all take for granted
Back then he would exclaim to anyone,
 And everyone, "I'm Tute" for cute
Later on has he grew, he became Mr. Awesome
I will always treasure our memories together
Yes, my Son, you were Tute, and you remain
Awesome!

D Everett Newell 5/3/2021

Thanks Saige Corey Newell, you are one of God's greatest gifts to me, I'll be forever Thankful

My Lucky Sherm

Oh, what a lucky Sherm
He was
A man of very small stature
One who possessed distinct
Magical qualities
Everything Sherm touched
Turned to gold,
Metaphorically speaking
He was a very lucky dude
Being worth his weight in riches
People sided up to him
Sometimes for nefarious reasons
Making it hard
For this potbellied guy to trust
He with the long bushy sideburns
Owning that mischievous
Toothless grin
Anyone,
Would want him by their side
Placing him there,
Would be a boast,
To all endeavor's
Any time he needed
My friend could disappear
And at a whim reappear
Also changing his size
Fitting anywhere he like
Dime like,
Now resting in my pocket

Take my word for it
I never went anywhere
Without me,
Lucky Sherm

D Everett Newell 11/11/2019

Saige Corey Newell

New England

On a warm early August morning
An adventure began
Driving off as one, a family united
Riding in a twelve-seat chariot
Taking the long winding road
Through New York finally reaching
The beautiful Vermont Mountains
Our first stop on this legendary trek
Ice cream, we all screamed, Ben and Jerry's
Whom among us, does not love
This sugary, icy, creamy treat

In the morning after breakfast
Assembled and once more
We hit the open highway
Arriving at our next destination
I've never seen a more moving sight
Waves crashing on rocks, over and over
The sea waters would not be denied
The numerous Gulls,
Dive bombing everywhere
Bar Harbor Maine, so much eye candy
A family again together
Watching, enjoying nature's canvas

Hitting the road again
On a backwards trend home
Drove through and stayed
In New Hampshire

The White Mountain ranges
And surrounding areas, were breathtaking
Large mountains, snow fed
Creeks and rivers glistened in the sun
The roads traveled were eye candy
The traveling company,
Made up of family was icing on the cake

A trip of legendary memory, through New England

D Everett Newell 11/15/2019

Nighttime Terrors

I can't sleep, can't relax
Wish I could shut my brain down
So many thoughts screaming to be heard
Why now, why me
I'm ready to end my day
Yet something has me working overtime
Every time I try and relax,
My thoughts speed up
SO trying and aggravating,
I want to sleep
Damn it, another hour gone
I just want to drift away
Need to get up early I need to sleep
Pleading almost, and trying once again
SO trying and aggravating,
I want to sleep
Damn it, another hour gone
Getting nowhere panic takes over
Tossing and turning, then fuming
Starting over again, calming down
Again to chasing that elusive sleep
SO trying and aggravating,
 I want to sleep
Damn it, another hour gone
Growing more weary by the hour
Fraught with apprehension
As day light comes
Finally giving up, getting up
I'm done for now

It has won the night
And I'm totally spent from
Fighting the nighttime terror's

D Everett Newell 5/2/2021

Monument at Gettysburg PA

Out of My Depth

We all have certain
Comfort zones,
Events and or people
We are never at ease with
Always trying to find balance
When we can't, nerves take over
Causing a rather stark
Constipation of the brain
People do the strangest things
Deriving from this affliction
Sometimes we laugh
In the face of danger
To flee or fight, is our right
We may shed tears
On hearing good news
Never a conclusive way
To understand the human brain
Complicated and hardwired
Explaining any further
Would show you, I'm
…Totally out of my depth

D Everett Newell 2/22/2021

Poet's Horror

What any poet wants
Truth be told, is to be heard
Writing needs a reading
Articulating emotional thoughts
Not every piece fits all
But every poem fits someone
A least that is the grand plan
When a poet gets no feedback
It's the proverbial 'Kiss of Death'
Rather constructive criticism
Than a perpetual indifference
So I beg, please reciprocate
Not in any tangible way
A dollar and cents way, but
Give the most important resource
The one of yourself
Time, interest, sharing
Help your favorite writer
Avoid a poet's horror

D Everett Newell 10/5/2021

Saturday Morning

A calm has come
The rush of the week, over
Sun rises on a quiet land
Birds gently chirping and peeping
Nary a soul walking around
The grass shines, glistens
Nature's lights burning off the dew
Yes, it's a fresh day begun anew
I feel light, unburdened
The Second of October
We've now passed the corner
Summer is now firmly behind
Fall is a good time on this planet
A time of change and transition
We who live here, repeat our four seasons
Much like a laundromat
Spin, cycle, dry, spin, cycle, dry
But here it's winter, spring, summer, fall
Tree leaves starting to show a change
Within weeks, they'll achieve royal hues
Then that cycle over, will drop and die
But this morning it's all very clear
This morning I'll drink it all in
On this morning I'll smile
Breathing deeply satisfied for now
On this Saturday morning

D Everett Newell 10/2/2021

Seven Pillars

Lucky I am, lucky was I
Born into a traditional family
Strong matriarch, loving patriarch
And the Seven Pillars of support
My Dad and his six siblings
Followed the teachings of their parents
Setting in stone a way of life
For me and my brother and cousins
We learned how to act
How to treat people with dignity
We learned about God
How to interact with Love
Music was everywhere
The family get togethers were large and loud
Lessons learned by watching them
Those Seven Pillars, because of them
My house, my kids' houses
Are built sturdy and strong
I owe everything I am
To those Seven Pillars

Dedicated to Aunts Jo, Emilie, Jesse, Mary and Uncles David and Harwood, and my Dad John

D Everett Newell 3/19/2021

Skeletons

My closet has them
Does yours?
No one leads
A perfect life
If we are honest
Even to the best of our intentions
We just are not
Perfect being's
We do try, then try some more
We humans
 are fraught with errors
These misjudgments
 can be mental or physical
 Actions, and more
We all have things
We've done, were not proud of
Albeit skeletons in our
Many'd Closets
We bury them over time
Forget them, or make amends
Since Eve ate the first apple
Adding to our trials and tribulations
Man's destiny
Is to be a flawed entity
I remain very sure
I have several Skeletons
In my personal closet

D Everett Newell 11/12/2019

Soldiers of The Civil War

Marching miles upon miles
In heavy woolen uniforms
In the best of times
Heavy, itchy and warm
Shoes that don't fit
Holes on the soles, blistery feet
Miserable most of the time
Now add the cold of winter
Ice, snow on trees
Glisten in the moonlight
Fires hard to light
Wood being wet, dry is hard to find
Walking through drifts, cold water puddles
Life is a daily mundane chore
Let alone fighting a war
Pushing animals at every step
Moving cannons and wagons
Hard to cook food, to find any
Yet spirits continue to soar
Hard to understand the
Soldiers of The Civil War

D Everett Newell 3/14/2021

Solemn Promises

To all we love, have loved, will love
WE give our solemn promises
To do our best to honor and love
Staying loyal to our friendships
Always embracing,
 All our shared memories
Praying we never,
 Let each other down
Being human, it is inevitable to error
Given enough chances,
We do and will mess up
Take those moments in stride
Remember the many laughs shared
All of our moments created
Being a pack animal,
WE no longer hunt together
Yet we do always long to be together
Naturally occurring warmth
 When huddled together
A constant feeling of belonging derived
From a familiar fellowship
Of man, woman and child

D Everett Newell 4/24/2021

Soup

By the bone, or by the can
Piping bubbling hot
Crackers or not
This meal warms us inside
Filling us somewhat
Sometimes it does not
But does it really quench our hunger
In some cases, our thirst
Depending on the mixture
We will rue, the day
Our stoves heat up
Melting an exciting elixir
Made with chicken or beef stock
Bisques and Chowders come at us
Vegetables and assorted meats
Crackers with the Chili
A mouth-watering treat
Adding cheese or onions
A party in a bowl
My mouth drooling
Thinking about my next
Big mug of soup!

D Everett Newell 11/11/2019

Sports Hurts

Loving competition
Flexing muscles
Me against you
Whose will is stronger
A contest to be contested
Both of us incrementally bested
I hit a run
You throw, then catch
Scoring matters, but winning
This ultimate will
Yours against mine
Matters the most, I can
Be victor, even if my team loses
But really, what importance it poses
The real struggle lies within
Knowing we did our best
We did not cower or wither
Even if no conquest
Participate fully, don't play in spurts
Go til you can't anymore
Sports hurts

D Everett Newell 10/2/2021

Sudden Loss

The pain we feel
Hurts like Hell
Over sudden loss
Especially when there is no
Explanation or reasoning of it
Why does that happen?
Some say, God's plan
But hard for us to accept
I guess the greater the pain
The bigger the hole in our life
Means that it was substantial
In or love and closeness
So many times
We are caught off guard
We can only remember
We can only move on
The absence can never be filled
Counting on distance and years
They dull the senses, and our emptiness
The pain we feel
Hurts like hell
Over our sudden loss

D Everett Newell 2/19/2021

Sun

It's mighty cold out
You can see a frothy breath
The sun is brilliant
Winter mornings are ravishing
My belief more intense
Than the summer rays
Gleaming off mounds of stubborn snow
Our yard glaciers shrinking
From the mighty strobe of light
The air clean, fresh, crisp
Cotton white puffs float
Amid the definitive blue sky
Glorious are these type of days
Winter's push toward spring
You can hear, feel our world
Beginning to engage once more
Yet still, it's mighty cold out
Seeing a still silhouetted frothy breath
So happy though, in our brilliant sun

D Everett Newell 3/7/2021

That's a Frustration

No one living portrayed in this piece
Shall be named
That's a Frustration
I offered my books to a female friend
Because of her eyesight she could not read them
That's a Frustration
Then offered to read them out loud
But my voice is gone and I cough continually
That's a Frustration
One person I know likes to put me down
Insinuating I'm not a real author
That's a Frustration
Some writings seem like a great idea
Yet when pen hits the paper, it's not
That's a Frustration
Many people that support me, which is appreciated
Although not sure they've read my words
That's a Frustration
I'd love to write more intensely
It's probably time to end
That's a Frustration

D Everett Newell 2/27/2021

The Flood, At the Dobbins House

Sitting at our assigned tables
Carefully looking over the menu
Fire crackled over the many fireplace
The aroma's, "to die for"
Smells of another world, an old world
From the time of Independence
Played within our senses
Of Sight, sound, smell
Period waitresses and worn cutlery
Having been there before
Many times, before, a bastion of warmth
Anticipation for Onion Soup climbed
Our favorite place to eat
Down in its bowels, in the tavern
Cool, dark, smells of centuries passed
Lucky, we dodged a torrential rain
Escaped to our place of comfort
…or did we? Water began to seep in
Slowly it creeped,
Over the brick and stone floor
Now a perpetual glistening mirror
To all kinds of flickering candlelight
Inevitable to our feet becoming wet
Onward this wet determined army moved
Much likened to,
 An Army of Blue of yesteryear
We sat, giving in
 To the unquestioned end
We were told, an event that has not happened

At least in twenty years of remembrance
Thus, a celebration for us
Luck sometimes is not realized in the moment
Another dear memory we just shared
So many made here at this place,
Forever forward known to us
As the great Gettysburg Flood
In our beloved Dobbins House

D Everett Newell Sept 9, 2021

The Grim Reaper Covid

2020, a year from hell
Our lives disrupted forevermore
Society had to separate
Not an easy task for pack species
Covid-19 rode in from China
As if Satan once more fell
Heaven opened up, down came he
And his hellion angels
That great red dragon
Breathing his sickness breath
That deathly chronic cough
Accompanied by chills
Shortness of breath
Taking 100,000's
Losing taste, smell
Acquiring a myriad of muscle and body aches
In our imagining of cruel deaths
We could not ever come this close
Surely it had the face
Of the robed skeleton, The Grim Reaper
One last effort, on a suffering humanity
A surge to separate our soul
From our physical bodies
Damn You Covid-19

D Everett Newell 10/6/2021

The Tough Mantel Of Life

When you get a call for help
From someone you deeply care about
But your choices are limited
In any meaningful way
What can you do
When you can't find a substantive answer
Hearing the pain in others voices
Wears upon your heart, troubling the soul
Trying everything from humor to tears
Hoping somehow to break thru
A formidable wall
All understanding disappearing at each hello
A person disappearing every hour of every day
Shared memories now one sided and obsolete
Praying for answer, knowing there are none
Can only stand by watch this play out
Yet you keep on thru the anger and confusion
Trying to connect again and again and again
People matter, their worth struggling for,
And completely giving them the compassion
They thru a long well lived life have earned
This is the tough mantle of life!

D Everett Newell 4/24/2021

This Mixed Jungle

Cement buildings, jutting out
Plastics holding all
Noise from man's machines
Hurts my senses
Nature has been pushed aside
An unnatural wake of gas-powered rides
So many people in such a small space
No wonder mountains made of human waste
Steel equipment replacing humans
Aided by their artificial intelligence
Scary to think how fragile we are
Skin, bones and water is man
A probability of losing our planet
Faces our future, can we stop its erosion
Or are we headed to a perpetual end
As long as we reign, we will hold on
Best we can, we continue to live
In this unbridled world
Caught in a web of this mixed jungle

D Everett Newell 2/14/2021

This Problem

Society has many problems
Sitting here today
Breaking news, again Breaks
Again, another place
Loses their innocence
After the latest school shooting
The anti-gun folks
Immediately rattle their chains
They suddenly
Are up in no arms
They as always blame the NRA
They blame all gun owners
Yet, the underlying problem
IS the fact,
If your dead set on killing
You will find a way
If not with a gun,
 with something else
Taking away guns is a band-aid
At best
We need to address
the Mental Health of people
Then maybe this insanity
Will finally be stopped
It is not a gun issue
And killing will not end
Till we address the root cause
Somehow, we have
Desensitized killing

Minimized how precious a life is
When we address these issues
There will be an end
To This problem!

D Everett Newell 11/15/2019

To Snack or Not

Snacks, unhealthy blows
To a dietary plan
Can't live without them
Shorten life if you do
That salt and sugar combo
Makes our tongues wag
Our brains light up
In anticipation
But beware we are told
Over and over again
The Health professionals
unified cry
Belly rolls form
Not from laughing
And are sure to follow
To snack or not
That is the question
Seemingly I am without
An answer!

D Everett Newell 11/15/2019

To

To see, hear, touch
Is liberating
To taste, smell
Is being alive
To make rash judgements
Is ignorant
To act dishonorably
Is without integrity
To mock, ignore, judge
Is Problematic
To them, they, it
Is without empathy
To you, me, all of us
Is inclusive
To smile, embrace with kindness
Is a bringing together
It's the right thing
We just have to!

D Everett Newell 11/11/2019

Travel Log 2021

Life is a roller coaster
Many ups, then downs
Curve after curve
Combined laughter and terror
Tears unabated from both
It's a futuristic trip
Built on memories from our past
A wild ride on soul's rocket
Firing full cylinders
Mostly planned, controlled
But then, the new times we have
Spontaneous fire taking us away
Breathtaking, illuminating, a virus
Viral, visceral, viciously moving
Would not change my path
Given choice, I'd still take this ride
I'd have no choice intrinsic
To being what and who I am
A trip for our ages
A life well lived
I stand, I live onward
Reporting from my Travel Log 2021

D Everett Newell 10/5/2021

Traveling Man

I love to travel
Beauty lies all around us
Been up and down the East Coast
To the Bahama Islands
Yet I'll never be satisfied

I've not seen the Mississippi River
Its power pushing paddle boats up and down

I've not seen the Alamo in Texas
Its memory etched in our history

I've not seen the Great Canyon
A natural wonder showing water's power

I've not seen the deserts of Arizona
The dry, flat, hot vastness of earth

I've not seen the Pacific Ocean
A huge body of undetermined horizons

I've not seen the Hawaiian volcanoes
Spewing the hot fiery lava

I love to travel
Beauty lies all around us
Been up and down the East Coast
But I'll never be done
I am a traveling man!

D Everett Newell 9/21/2021

Trees, Now Gone

It rips out my heart
The Chainsaws
I hear them out back
Their hideous sound
Tearing into our trees
Singing their loud grinding song
The Satanic Ash Borer
Ended their life,
One after another they came down
Now just a pile of kindling
Only silver lining
Is their death supplies the fuel
To heat several family's homes
I cringe now
Looking out my window
Seeing the animals
Scurrying around
No homes to be found
Their old haunts now gone
We must go on
Just like the squirrels
With our Trees now gone

D Everett Newell 11/15/2019

Trick or Treater

Written on Hallows Eve
I sit in my home
Waiting on the scary minions
To come to our barren door
Then the anticipation ends
With a ring of the bell
And steady loud knocks
The night's onslaught has begun
We have our bowl
of sweets at the ready
Small comics too
The Great candy grab is underway
This yearly event is on
Costumes of every type
Some scary some funny
Some out of this world
A parade of children of all ages
And of various size
Nothing will stop this charge now
Not the cold drizzly rain
Or the darkness of the night
The setting on a whole
Takes an eerie form
Then nothing, it is over
We were lucky this time
We had far more Treaters,
Then Tricks!

D Everett Newell 11/15/2019

Type This

I'm sorry, I said type this
Seems you can't hear well
The clickety clack of my type
Will wake you up, get your attention
Oh what kind am I, you ask
I am bold I am fresh
Yet to many nuisances
To button or pigeonhole me
Your turn, what type are you
Well excuse me, that is just rude
I think you can spare a moment
To indulge my hard work
Its really the simplest question
Turn about is the fairest of plays
Is it not, I ask you
The reality of this exercise
Or actually the reality of everything
Is to build a dialog,
A form of communication
Thereby we get to know one another
We build some kind of human bond
Or this will be a complete waste of effort
Your time and mine, with no interchange
So let me start once more
As I begin again, to Type This

D Everett Newell 4/27/2021

Vestibule

To the vestibule
My channel to the world
I put on my socks
Slip into comfortable
Ragged, smelly sneakers
I hear the wind charged air
Rattling my doors
Being that insult to my senses
This antechamber, a last vestige
Of warmth, protection, and safety
Reaching for that doorknob
Turning it slowly, surely
Pushing an opening
Against the world, out I walk
All hell is blowing about
Seizing upon this moment
Shrugging my shoulders
Thinking, 'Nope, I'm not'
And I return
To where I started
The Vestibule

D Everett Newell 10/4/2021

Wallet or A Murse

My red leather satchel
Hangs around my neck
Holding all that is scared
Money various methods
of identification
Always wear I can view it
Hangling and dangling center
Preventing its removal
No slick of hand or force
Can take it from me
I have had many of these
In many fashions
I have had many comments
Thru the years,
Making fun of me
That only makes me stronger
More committed
It has come in Red, Black or Brown
The colors of the world
I call it my man bag
The burning question
Of these riches holding sack
Is it a wallet, a manly Purse?
Or simply said, a murse!

D Everett Newell 11/13/2019

What a Mouth on Her

A lady in the making
Dressed in her shiny dress
Bauble and sparkles
High heel shoes
Perfume wafts up
Permeates all the air around
She makes a Grand Entrance
Self-appointed Royalty
In her head a symphony plays
Glaring she stares at all
No one dares make eye contact
Then it happens
She opens her red painted lips
And a voice shrieks, loudly outward
One of the most vile creatures
Put on this earth
Despite all the frills and dressing
Nothing but profanity rolled out
This proves you can dress her up
But you never know
What may happen because
We've come to know
What a mouth on her

D Everett Newell 11/15/2019

When Dear Friend's Disappears

I know you are alive
But for some reason,
 your gone
I don't think its personal
But, your gone
Why, there is no explanation
Just gone, and don't respond
Figured we'd grow old together
And that does suck, getting old
Have I said your gone
I try and I try, in fact I wont stop
Made a moral agent agreement
We would be friends thru thick & thin
Yet you are gone, no notice
I do worry about you and I wonder
Why you climb within yourself
Isolation is its own prison
We need people more then ever
So what possessed you
To withdraw, stop reengage
I Promise,
that when you take a stand
Here I remain, to help
Anyway possible, please
Note, I just hate
When dear friends disappear

D Everett Newell 4/26/2021

Whimsy

Do you ever just do
No thinking just acting
Just let yourself go
I mean with no thought,
No apprehension.
Just close off your brain
To all outside debilitating fears
Live in the moment
Come on let it rip
I would advise you
To not be standing
 on a four lane highway
To not be hanging
Over a 400 foot cliff
To not be dating
Two women at once
And don't quit your job
Without another source
 of income lined up
But by all means
Just let it rip
Go for it, as I often say
What is life without Whimsy?

D Everett Newell 4/26/2021

Who is Albert Woolson, PT 2

I'm so glad you asked
You did, I'm sure
He became a symbol
For an ERA long gone
Albert was the last Civil War Veteran
Being that last survivor
He had represented his generation well
Participated in their Great War
Unlike the many, he lived to tell about it
Albert died in 1956
Serendipity at work
As we shared three years
On this planet
Hard to believe, but true
Mr. Woolson was the last
Yes, the last Civil War Vet
Enlisting in 1864, as a drummer boy
Just a young lad of fourteen
Drumming for the 1st Minnesota Heavy Artillery
He never saw the elephant
Being discharged in 1865
Yet he became a prominent
Veteran leading GAR
The Grand Army of the Republic
In 1953 I was born
And this vet became
A Senior Vice Commander
You can visit his memorial
A statue outside the

Near The High-Water Mark, Gettysburg, PA
Fronting what is now,
The Soldiers Cemetery
This was Albert Woolson
Now you know.

D Everett Newell 9/23/2021

Saige Corey Newell

Wondering Mind

Focus remains a bit slow
Even somewhat out of tilt
Perceptions aren't to be believed
What has suddenly come over me
My emotions are a merry-go-round
I feel great, then sad, then
Here comes great again
I so want off this crazy wheel
Life is hard, harder yet
When thoughts are jagged
Fragmented, or nonsensical
I'm OK most of the time
The time I'm not, suck
Thinking to myself is not
My best friend, or best outcome
Fighting all the time
To override consequences
Determined by the wondering mind

D Everett Newell 5/18/2021

Would Not

How do we get to where we are
I mean, why did we choose,
Certain paths and decisions,
That lead one, then a life lived
Making good ones and bad,
Go into who we all are

If we could go back,
Pick different routes, would we
Would we be different people
Or are we predestined on the outcome,
Living is all by chance

Is something larger at play here
Having no answers
But it does boggle my mind.
How about you
Have you given much thought

A bigger question
Could we pick a different route
I would not, I would not
Take a chance on losing
All my family and friends
All the memories, experiences
Simply, I would NOT!

D Everett Newell 2/26/2021

Yellow Balloon

The Yellow Balloon
Bounding into my yard
Upon green blades of grass
Blown slowly by the wind
To the asphalt beyond

Then off one tree and another
Weightlessly it continued
My gaze was stolen
As I watched its magical trek

Where did you come from?
Better yet, where will you end?

Good-bye and Thanks Yellow Balloon!

D Everett Newell 9/1/2021

Yonder

Love nature. It's all encompassing.

In the winter
We have snow white drifts
On great days
Brilliant sun, soft floating clouds
At night, deer around the bird feeder
A fox running his route
Squirrels scampering, looking for food
Love nature. It's all encompassing.

In the spring
We have the manied trees returning to life
Our gray brown yards turning green
Hearing the Canadian geese on their return
Creek bed filling, then rushing
From the now browning snow melting
Birds of all types singing
Love nature. It's all encompassing.

In the summer
People return to daily walks
Bonfires emit their smell at night
The stars never shine more brilliantly
Picnics and gatherings abound
Summertime sports, festivals, music return
Our world is simply full again
Love nature. It's all encompassing.

In the fall
Leaves start their color pallet
Nuts dropping from trees
Pumpkins bursting
Halloween ghouls thirsting
Our field resplendent in abundance
Of foods that feed us
Love nature. It's all encompassing.
All that's required is to look Yonder.

D Everett Newell 2/20/2021

Slugger

At three you could
Yes, you could
Hitting, throwing as
You tracked the balls
We knew you'd be special
Every year since
Improving at every level
Confident, experienced
You have become at a
Still very young age
A force to be reckoned with
Our pride in you
Is beyond expression
Now at thirteen, you
Yes, you
Hit, throw, track all balls
You are the one
A polished one
My own special Slugger

D Everett Newell 10/16/2021

For Ella

I am, The Author, D Everett Newell

My name is Dennis Everett Newell; I am called in no certain order, Denny, Den, Big D, D Everett, and Dennis. It's funny, but I can usually tell by how someone calls my name, what time in my life we shared. I guess there are many layers to a life that has now spanned 68 years. My middle name, Everett, has been passed down in our family since the Civil War. My great-great-grandfather's name was Darius Newell, who named his son Silas Everett Newell, my great-grandfather. He in turn named his son John Everett Newell, my grandfather, who then in turn named my dad, John Everett Newell Jr. My dad named me Dennis Everett Newell, and my son is Corey Everett Newell.

Poetry, and my stories are my way of slaying the inner dragons within my mind, thus allowing my inner feelings and passions to escape – my relief valve if you will! I draw on my own personal inspiration from my assimilations and experience of my life lived. Experiences that I have taken then shaped and formed into stories and poems. Moments garnered from all people I have interacted with, during all these years of living. I am from a family with a long history of wordsmiths. Within these pages, I try not to let down those that came before me, and to pass a standard to those who will come after. Taking on this family mantle, I do so with pride and to the best of my meager abilities.

I now live in Western New York, an area that if you don't like the weather, wait 24 hours and it will change. The people that live here are tough, able, caring and resilient. I originated from the hills of Pennsylvania - a small town, Falls Creek, in the foothills of the Allegheny Mountain chain. Within my family heritage you will find lumberjacks, coal miners, and people of every vocation. You will also find warmth, loyalty and support. This family is the most loving and lovely family a young boy and now late middle-aged man could possibly ever hope for.

My passions are, in no particular order, writing, photography, paranormal, history (Civil War and WW II), music, poetry, sports, computers, I am a people watcher. I am you see, an everyday man, with the same everyday thoughts as all of you. I hope with all of my heart, something you read in this book will touch you. I hope you can pause and maybe reflect on your own life and world. My Dad taught me very early on, be a 'stop and smell the roses' man!

Thank YOU.

D Everett Newell, the Big D

To reach the Big D, his email is Bygd1@aol.com, You can find all Eleven of my books for purchase on Amazon, Cyberwit.Net, or by emailing me personally,

And now you can listen to my words and my other favorite Poets on The: Podcast, Poet D Everett Newell!